Asia

Monika Davies

Consultants

Kerry Shannon, Ph.D.
Assistant Professor of History
California State University, Dominguez Hills

Roger B. Han, M.A.
Freelance Educator and Business Consultant

Mab Huang, Ph.D.
Political Science Professor

Brian Allman
Principal
Upshur County Schools, West Virginia

Publishing Credits

Rachelle Cracchiolo, M.S.Ed., *Publisher*
Emily R. Smith, M.A.Ed., *SVP of Content Development*
Véronique Bos, *Vice President of Creative*
Dani Neiley, *Editor*
Fabiola Sepulveda, *Series Graphic Designer*

Image Credits: p.7 Getty Images/Dorling Kindersley; p.8 Alamy/The Picture Art Collection; p.9 (top) Wiki Commns/Atharva-Veda Samhitā second half; p.10 (top) Shutterstock/John Theodor; p.16 Getty Images/Baona; p.18 Getty Images/Heritage Images; p.20 Alamy/Robert Gilhooly; p.22 Library of Congress [LC-USZ62-66033]; pp. 24–25 Alamy/Lou-Foto; p. 25 (bottom) Shutterstock/Akramalrasny; p.26 Shutterstock/MACH Photos; p.27 (middle) Shutterstock/Stanislav Samoylik; p.27 (bottom) Shutterstock/Nick Fox; all other images from iStock and/or Shutterstock

Library of Congress Cataloging-in-Publication Data

Names: Davies, Monika, author.
Title: Asia / Monika Davies.
Description: Huntington Beach, CA : Teacher Created Materials, 2023. | Includes index. | Audience: Ages 8-18 | Summary: "Asia takes up a lot of space on a map. It's home to over half our global population! Asia has a long history-and diverse geography. In the last decades, Asia has seen major changes and growth. Are you ready to explore this vast and varied continent?"-- Provided by publisher.
Identifiers: LCCN 2022038401 (print) | LCCN 2022038402 (ebook) | ISBN 9781087695174 (paperback) | ISBN 9781087695334 (ebook)
Subjects: LCSH: Asia--Juvenile literature.
Classification: LCC DS5 D385 2023 (print) | LCC DS5 (ebook) | DDC 950--dc23/eng/20220824
LC record available at https://lccn.loc.gov/2022038401
LC ebook record available at https://lccn.loc.gov/2022038402

Shown on the cover is Kyoto, Japan.

TCM | Teacher Created Materials

5482 Argosy Avenue
Huntington Beach, CA 92649
www.tcmpub.com
ISBN 978-1-0876-9517-4

Table of Contents

Exploring Asia

Asia takes up a lot of space on a map. It's easily the world's largest continent. Billions of people live in these 48 countries. Three territories are also part of Asia. Asia is home to over half our global population! These countries and territories have many differences. Each one comes with its own history and culture.

Typically, Asia is split into large regions. East Asia is one region. China is one of the most well-known East Asian countries. South Asia is the next region. It includes India, Pakistan, and Nepal. Central Asia is a region divided into five countries, including Kyrgyzstan. Western Asia includes many different countries. Some of them are considered to be in the Middle East, such as Iraq and Saudi Arabia. North Asia includes Siberia, a region of land that mostly belongs to Russia. Southeast Asia is the last region. This book focuses on all of the regions except Southeast Asia.

There is a lot to see and learn about Asia. Are you ready to explore this vast and varied continent?

Guiyang, China

Agra, India

Astana, Kazakhstan

Dubai, United Arab Emirates

RUSSIA

KAZAKHSTAN

MONGOLIA

Lake Baikal

Black Sea

GEORGIA
ARMENIA AZERBAIJAN

Caspian Sea

KYRGYZSTAN

TURKEY

TURKMENISTAN

UZBEKISTAN

TAJIKISTAN

NORTH KOREA

Sea of Japan

JAPAN

LEBANON
PALESTINE (ISRAEL)
SYRIA
IRAQ

KUWAIT

IRAN

AFGHANISTAN

CHINA

SOUTH KOREA

JORDAN

BAHRAIN
QATAR
UNITED ARAB EMIRATES

PAKISTAN

NEPAL

BHUTAN

North Pacific Ocean

SAUDI ARABIA

Gulf of Oman

OMAN

Arabian Sea

INDIA

BANGLADESH

MYANMAR (BURMA)

TAIWAN

Red Sea

YEMEN

Gulf of Aden

Bay of Bengal

LAOS

MACAU (CHINA)
HONG KONG (CHINA)

Philippine Sea

Indian Ocean

SRI LANKA

THAILAND

CAMBODIA

VIETNAM

South China Sea

PHILIPPINES

MALDIVES

MALAYSIA

SINGAPORE

I N D O N E S I A

TIMOR-LESTE

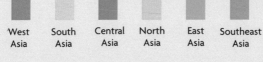

West
Asia

South
Asia

Central
Asia

North
Asia

East
Asia

Southeast
Asia

A Brief History

Asian countries do not share a single, unified history. Every country has a history of its own. Each one has a story to tell. Years of history in Asia can roughly be divided into three periods. Let's look at some historical highlights.

First Civilizations

Humans once roamed the world as hunters and gatherers. They were always on the move. They hunted and fished to feed their families.

Then, the **nomadic** habits of humans began to shift. People who used to wander widely started to settle. Instead of hunting, they turned to farming to grow their food. These groups of people formed societies. Cities started to take shape. And humans began to create written languages to tell their stories.

Civilizations were large groups of people. These groups shared ways of living and working. Asia is home to the world's earliest civilizations. Mesopotamia was the first. This area was in what is now modern-day Iraq. This society began around 3500 BCE.

A thousand years then passed. Another society emerged. This was known as the Indus civilization. It was located in the Indus River valley. This area was in what is now present-day Pakistan. Around this time, Chinese civilization also began.

5,000 Years of Stories

People have not always had history books. Writing was only invented 5,000 years ago! This was around 3200 BCE.

Cuneiform was an ancient writing form.

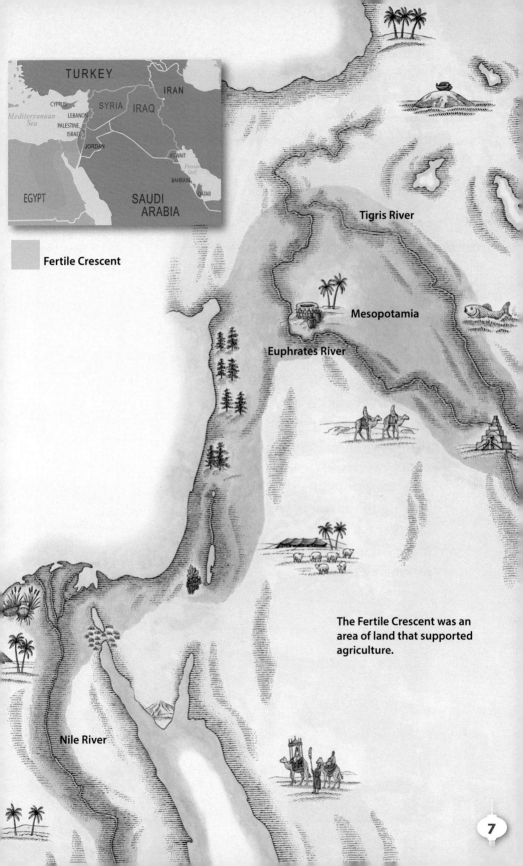

TURKEY

CYPRUS

SYRIA

LEBANON

PALESTINE

ISRAEL

JORDAN

Mediterranean
Sea

EGYPT

IRAN

IRAQ

KUWAIT

Persian
Gulf

BAHRAIN

QATAR

SAUDI
ARABIA

Fertile Crescent

Tigris River

Mesopotamia

Euphrates River

The Fertile Crescent was an
area of land that supported
agriculture.

Nile River

Some civilizations grew. Others **collapsed** over time. Different cultures began to form across Asia. Three cultures took on great importance during this time. These early groups of people set the foundation in Asia. They achieved great things.

Chinese civilization took hold in East Asia. The Shang **dynasty** is the first recorded dynasty. People lived in China before this time, but this time period is special. It was the first to be documented in history. This dynasty started around 1600 BCE. It ended hundreds of years later. Agriculture was important during this time. Many people worked as farmers. They grew crops. They also used an advanced calendar system. They made advancements in astronomy and math.

first emperor of the Shang Dynasty

Say What?

Hundreds of languages are spoken throughout Asia. Yes, *hundreds*! China's official language is Mandarin Chinese. In parts of southwest Asia, you are most likely to hear Arabic. In India, Hindi is the main language. Many people in Asia also speak Russian, English, or French.

In South Asia, the Indus civilization began to end. The Vedic period followed. This period is important in religious history. It is especially important in Hinduism. The oldest sacred texts were written during this time. The texts are called the *Vedas*. They were written between 1200 and 1500 BCE.

The Arab peoples lived in southwest Asia. Some Arabs were nomadic. This means they traveled. They did not stay in one place for very long. On the Arabian Peninsula, they herded their animals across the desert. Other Arabs stayed near oases. These are places in the desert where water is found. They grew dates and grains. Their culture became a key part of southwest Asia.

page from one volume of the *Vedas*

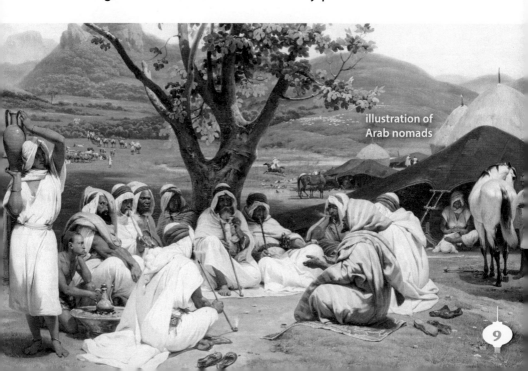

illustration of Arab nomads

Independence

For many centuries, Europeans controlled most of Asia. They controlled colonies across the land. The people in the colonies could not have their own governments. But this began to change after World War II. Starting in 1945, the map of Asia began to shift. Asian countries started to **regain** their independence. For instance, British rule came to an end in India. This happened in 1947.

In 1949, a civil war ended in China. This led to the rise of a **communist** government. The Korean War started soon after. This war ended in division. Korea split into two countries: North Korea and South Korea. A communist government leads North Korea.

Birthplace of Religions

Asia is where the first civilizations began. This is also true for many religions. Some call Asia the "birthplace of all major religions." A few major religions that are practiced throughout Asia include Buddhism, Hinduism, Judaism, Christianity, and Islam.

Torah scroll

Altering the Map

Asia's structure has shifted throughout the years. A lot of change has occurred, especially in the last few decades. One of the biggest changes to the continent happened in the 1990s.

In the 1900s, a country called the Soviet Union was the largest country in the world. The Soviet Union spread across Asia and Europe. It was made up of 15 republics that were controlled under one government. It was one of the most powerful countries in the world. In 1991, the Soviet Union broke up. When it broke up, each republic became its own country. This changed the map of Asia.

flag of the Soviet Union

Arctic Ocean

Laptev Sea

East Siberian Sea

republics of the former Soviet Union

RUSSIA

Sea of Okhotsk

NORTH KOREA

Sea of Japan

SOUTH KOREA

NGOLIA

NORTH KOREA

Sea of Japan

SOUTH KOREA

INA

Pacific Ocean

Geographic Features

Asia is a land of diverse geography. The continent is known for having both high mountains and vast flatlands. There are five main physical regions in Asia. Let's look first at the places with higher **elevations**.

High Mountains

Asia is famous for its mountain systems. First, the continent has the highest summit on the planet. Mount Everest is part of the Himalayas. This mountain range runs through northern India. It also covers most of Nepal and Bhutan.

The Tian Shan Mountains sit between two countries. Kyrgyzstan is on one side. China is on the opposite side. This mountain range has towering peaks. It also has miles of glaciers.

The Ring of Fire

Large tectonic plates sit on the earth's crust. When the plates grind together, earthquakes occur. Volcanic eruptions can also occur. The Pacific Ocean sits on the Pacific Plate. Rimming the plate's edge is the Ring of Fire. This is a horseshoe-shaped region where plates grind together often. Volcanoes and earthquakes happen frequently here. Almost 20 percent of the world's earthquakes happen in Japan. This is because of the country's closeness to the Ring of Fire.

Farther north are the Ural Mountains. The steep peaks draw a line between Russia and Kazakhstan. Some of the world's oldest mountains are found here. They are likely 250 million years old!

Vast Plateaus

Plateaus are huge areas of flat land. These landforms are at higher elevations, like mountains. But plateaus are characterized by their flatness.

The vast Iranian Plateau crosses three different Asian countries. This includes Iran, Afghanistan, and Pakistan. The Deccan Plateau goes across a large part of southern India. The Tibetan Plateau is playfully nicknamed "the roof of the world." This landform spans several countries. This includes China, Nepal, and India. It's the world's largest and highest plateau.

Tibetan Plateau and the Himalayas

Plains and Deserts

Around 75 percent of Asia is made of mountains and plateaus. It's a continent of high elevations. But the Asian mainland also includes low plains. Made of level ground, these areas often have wide valleys. Rivers flow through these low regions.

In central Russia, a plain dominates the landscape. It is called the West Siberian Plain. It is a large area of flat land. Big swamps are found across this land.

The Rub' al-Khali is a vast desert. It is one of the driest areas on the planet. Notably, it is also home to large amounts of **petroleum**. The desert mostly stretches across southeastern Saudi Arabia. It also covers parts of Yemen and Oman. The United Arab Emirates also has a piece of this desert.

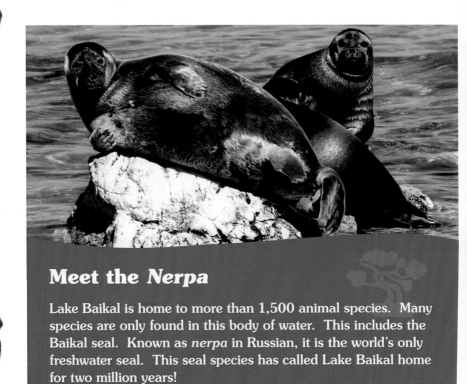

Meet the *Nerpa*

Lake Baikal is home to more than 1,500 animal species. Many species are only found in this body of water. This includes the Baikal seal. Known as *nerpa* in Russian, it is the world's only freshwater seal. This seal species has called Lake Baikal home for two million years!

Qutang Gorge,
Yangtze River, China

Water Flow

Asia has an **abundance** of lakes and rivers. The Caspian Sea is the world's largest inland body of water. It is found in central Asia. Several countries border this immense body of water. Lake Baikal is another famous lake. Baikal is in southern Russia. It is the world's deepest—and oldest—freshwater lake.

Noteworthy Asian rivers include the Yangtze River and Indus River. The Yangtze weaves through China. The river's water comes from the glaciers of the Tibetan Plateau. Meanwhile, the Indus River defines southern Asia. For centuries, it has been a source of water for farming on the Indus Valley plains.

oil pumps in China

Natural Resources

In Asia, the use of natural resources is linked to **decolonization**. For years, many Asian countries could not control or use their resources. Colonizing nations controlled them instead.

Asia is well-known for its minerals. Many of these are used for fuel. These include coal, petroleum, and natural gas. Southwest Asia produces most of the world's petroleum. China and Russia are major coal producers.

China and India both have large iron and steel industries. Iron ore is a key mineral for much of the world. It is a core part of steel production. Steel helps people build roads, railways, and buildings.

City Ranks

Around 55 percent of the world's population lives in cities. Over time, more and more people have moved from rural to urban settings in Asia. Some of the world's largest cities are found there. This includes Beijing (China), Tokyo (Japan), Seoul (South Korea), and Delhi (India).

Cultural Geography

Asia's geography is diverse. This diversity also extends to the people who live in Asia. Western Asia is home to Arabs and Jewish people. Turkish people and other groups also live there. Indian people and Pakistanis live in South Asia. Central Asia is where Kazakhs and many others live. Chinese, Japanese, and Korean peoples live in East Asia. Of course, many other people live in these regions as well. Many different groups of people call this area home.

Asia is a huge continent. There isn't one way to define its geography or people. It is a landmass rich in variety.

Girls carry water from a well in India.

the largest open-air market in Jerusalem, Israel

Economics in Asia

It is tricky to pinpoint the strength of Asia's economies. Many economists point to the overall economy of Asia as being strong and continually growing.

There are Asian countries with **flourishing** economies. These countries have access to a high degree of wealth. This includes countries such as Japan. Other Asian countries are struggling. These countries are still working to grow their economies. Let's explore why these economic differences exist.

The Role of Agriculture

Many people in rural areas work in agriculture. Rice is a food staple for most people. About 90 percent of the world's rice comes from Asia. Corn and wheat are also grown in Asia.

The Sea Life

The fishing industries in Japan and Russia are Asia's biggest and most advanced. Fishing is also a large industry in China and India. Seafood is consumed throughout Asia. It is especially popular in East Asia. This includes shrimp, lobster, octopus, and squid. Many different kinds of fish, including salmon and tuna, are eaten, too.

Many people in China and India work as farmers. Especially in Southeast Asia, people work as **subsistence farmers**. These farmers grow enough food for the people in their homes. If there are crops left over, they sell them for further income. Or, they can exchange them for other goods.

Trade

Natural resources are found in many places across Asia. Trade with other countries boosts the economy of each region. Mining is a big industry across the continent. Coal, natural gas, and other minerals are mined. Trees and bamboo are chopped down. Clothing and other textiles are made from cotton or wool. These goods are **exports** that are sold to other countries.

rice farming

The Role of Industrialization

There are large **income gaps** in Asia. This leads to great **inequality**. The reasons behind this are complex. Industrialization is a key term here. It refers to the building and operation of factories and businesses in an area. Some Asian economies are among the most industrialized. Taiwan is one of them. So are South Korea, Japan, and Singapore. They produce and sell many products. For instance, Japan produces a high number of cars. This is one of Japan's major exports.

Industrial growth is often tied to cities. Large companies and more job opportunities can be found in cities. Jobs in the service industry are common. Jobs in manufacturing, or production, are popular, too.

car factory in Japan

Mumbai, India

Rural vs. Urban

People from rural areas have started moving to larger cities. They move in hopes of an improved life. Millions of Asian people have relocated. But the cities lack enough jobs and housing for all. As a result, some cities are becoming overcrowded.

Asia's next decades will keep bringing great change. New technology may increase job opportunities in cities. And the populations of rural and urban areas will continue to shift.

The Role of Fossil Fuels

Western Asia is home to the largest deposits of oil and natural gas on the planet. Saudi Arabia's petroleum exports make up most of its economy. Petroleum accounts for almost 70 percent of its total exports. But fossil fuels are a major factor in climate change. How might these exports change in the future?

Civics and Government

Asia is made of citizens from nearly 50 countries. A government leads each country. Governments are meant to serve their citizens. But people can disagree with what kind of government works best. Let's examine what that means in Asia.

Democratic Freedoms

A democracy is a system of government. The word has Greek origins. It means "rule by the people." In a democracy, everyone has equal rights. There are free elections. Free media is prioritized. People feel at ease to speak up about issues. For some people, this freedom is a top civic value.

Some Asian countries have democracies. South Korea is a democracy. So are Japan and India. But every government is different. Freedoms are defined differently from place to place.

A Korean man votes in South Korea's first democratic election in 1948.

Communism

Communism is another system of government. The goal of communism is to share wealth with all citizens. In this system, everyone works to build wealth. People will receive only what they need. Citizens do not own factories or anything that helps them make goods. Rather, the government owns it all.

In theory, the aim of communism is to have a classless society. This way, everyone can be at an equal standing. Everyone shares their wealth.

Elections in India

India is home to one of the world's largest populations. This means there is a huge number of people who are able to vote. In 2019, around 900 million people could cast votes in the national election. There were one million polling stations across the country to make room for everyone!

Museum of the Communist Party in Beijing, China

China's government has been called a "one-party government." The Chinese Communist Party (CCP) leads the country. The CCP once owned all Chinese businesses. But now, people can run their own companies. This has led to China's economic growth.

Present-day communism looks different than it once did. There are more economic freedoms. But there are still limits in place.

Authoritarian Power

Authoritarian power is placed with only one leader or government. Freedoms are limited. People in power do not always follow laws in place. They may curb freedom of speech. Citizens often cannot vote for who they want to lead them. And leaders are also not easily replaced. This kind of power is rising in parts of Asia.

Leadership shapes a country's future. And countries shape their continent's future. What's next for civics in Asia? On this front, a lot is likely to change in the coming years.

a protest in Yemen

Arab Spring

In late 2010 and 2011, the Arab Spring happened. This was a period of pro-democracy protests. People started to protest against their governments. They protested in favor of democracy. Protests occurred in some countries in west Asia and North Africa. The movement started in Tunisia. It quickly spread to west Asia. Protests occurred in Bahrain, Yemen, and Syria. Some protests resulted in governmental changes. Some government leaders were dismissed.

A Diverse Continent

The main theme for Asia is diversity. Asian countries differ in how they govern themselves. Their landscapes vary widely. While their histories overlap, each Asian country has its own story to share.

Asia, as a whole, is hard to categorize. It is a **kaleidoscope** of cultures. Different groups of people call each country home. Many are facing unique challenges. Some countries are growing in strength and wealth. Others are still struggling to overcome poverty.

Life looks different for someone in China compared to someone in Israel. Life in Japan is different from life in Russia. It's key to remember this wide range of experiences across the land. There is much to understand and explore on this continent.

A lot has changed in the last century for Asia. Decolonization began. Democracy rose but may now be falling. Economies started to soar and are still climbing. The next decades will only see further change for Asia.

Over 60 percent of the world's population lives in Asia. This number will keep growing over time. Asia is a continent to watch. It will have a large role in directing our global future.

Osaka, Japan

fisher in China

port in Tel Aviv, Israel

Dhampus, Nepal

Climate Change in Asia

Many people in Asia live in **coastal** cities. Climate change
is leading to higher sea levels. Experts believe this will lead
to more floods and typhoons, or ocean storms. This will
affect people near the sea. People in Asia may be at the
greatest risk when it comes to climate change.

Map It!

It's time to map out a section of the world's largest continent. Grab a friend or two to collaborate with, and make a political map.

1. Choose a region of Asia covered in this book for your group's map-making:

   - East Asia
   - South Asia
   - Central Asia
   - West Asia
   - North Asia

2. Research which Asian countries are in your selected region. Write a list of the countries.

3. Using a large sheet of paper, sketch outlines of different countries in your selected region. Label each country.

4. Look up each country's capital city. Draw a star to pinpoint each country's capital on your map. Label each star with the capital's name.

5. Are there major oceans or rivers in your selected region? Label any major bodies of water in your selected region.

6. Look up the population numbers for each country. How many people live in each country? Write the total number next to each country's name.

Dal Lake in Srinagar, India

Omsk, Russia

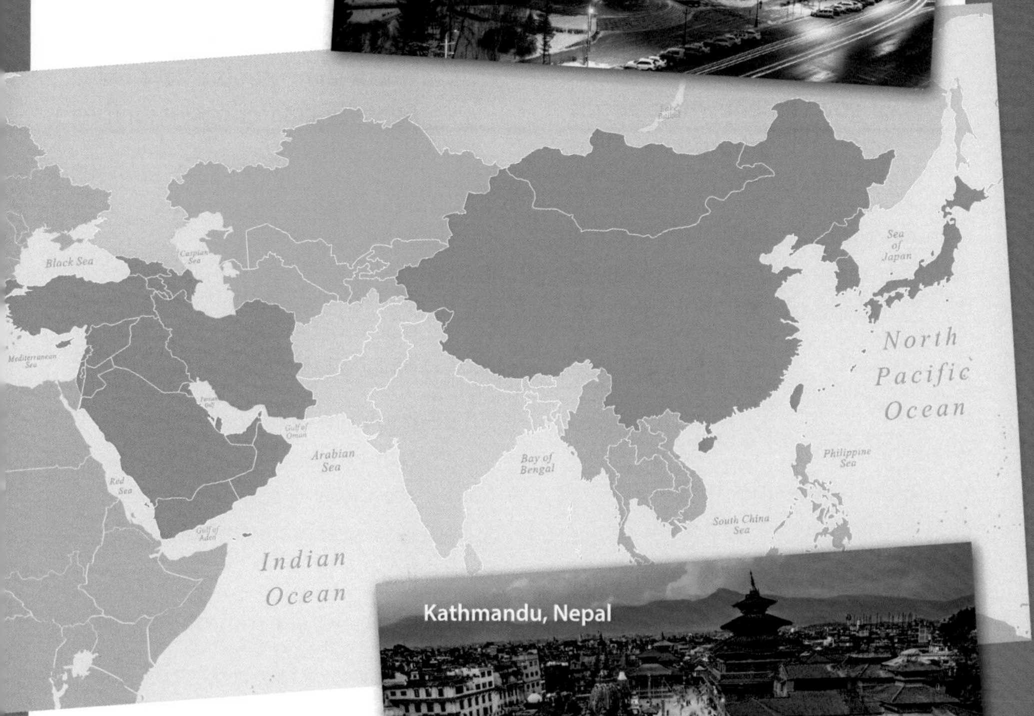

Black Sea

Caspian
Sea

Mediterranean
Sea

Sea
of
Japan

North
Pacific
Ocean

Gulf of
Oman

Arabian
Sea

Red
Sea

Gulf of
Aden

Bay of
Bengal

Philippine
Sea

South China
Sea

Indian
Ocean

Kathmandu, Nepal

Beijing, China

Glossary

abundance—a huge amount of something

coastal—bordering the ocean

collapsed—failed or broke down completely

communist—relating to a type of government where goods and means of production are publicly owned

decolonization—the process of making a colony or country independent and free

dynasty—a powerful group or family who rules over a country for a long time

elevations—the heights of things above sea level

exports—products that are sent to another state or country to be sold there

flourishing—quite successful

income gaps—significant differences between the amount of money that different groups or individuals have

inequality—an unfair situation in which some people have more rights or greater opportunities than others

kaleidoscope—a diverse collection

nomadic—moving from place to place instead of living in one place all the time

petroleum—a type of oil that comes from underneath the ground and can be used to make gasoline and other products

regain—to get something again

subsistence farmers—people who grow crops to meet their own needs

Seema Malaka temple in Colombo, Sri Lanka

Index

Learn More!

Life looks different for people across Asia. And life for a woman in Iran looks different from life for a woman in Japan. Nasrin Sotoudeh is an Iranian lawyer who fights for women's rights. She has spent time as a political prisoner. But she is committed to helping others.

- Research Sotoudeh's life.

- Create a brochure to share information about her. Answer each question on a panel of the brochure: What is her story? What issues does she care about? Where is she now?

- For the other panels, include pictures of her. You can also add quotations from her.

Yazd, Iran